Country Painting 101

Country painting for beginners

BIO

My name is Francesca and I am 27 years old, I live in Vicenza Italy with my husband Eric and our three furballs Minu', Midnight and Maat, I am a very social and friendly person and since I was little I always had a very strong passion for crafting, things like patchwork, painting,cross stitching and basically all that can be considered "crafting", about 4 years ago I discovered thanks to my frend Mirka the art of "Country painting" , It is an artistic discipline that impassions me a lot, and for this reason after some of my friends asked me to learn this technique, I started organizing monthly courses here in Vicenza to paint project of my creations; I have opened my own blog francescascountrypainting.com meeting many fellow painters/crafters and have now decided to publish this country painting manual.

And after this little intro i only have one question for you all ……………… ready to start painting?

With love

Francesca

CHAPTER 1

Materials

Country painting is a fantastic technique that will allow you to decorate or re use many type of surfaces, such as tin, wood, glass, ceramic and even cloth. In this book I will explain the bases of this technique and will also add two of my own patterns for you to practice with.

First of all let's begin by talking about the tools you will need:

Brushes

Good brushes are essential! A good brush makes all the difference; most of the good quality brushes are made with natural bristles, there is a difference in price from the synthetic bristles but it is worth it. On websites such as hofcraft.com or joanne.com you will be able to buy all the brushes needed for country painting and all the other materials needed as well. As brushes are so important, it is also important to understand how to take care of them: after every painting session, clean you brushes with neutral soap and carefully rinse them with water, then place them on a towel until they are dry. Acrylic colors tend to dry quickly, which means that if some paint remains on the bristles of your brush, it will glue the bristles together and you will most likely have to throw your brush away and buy a new one.

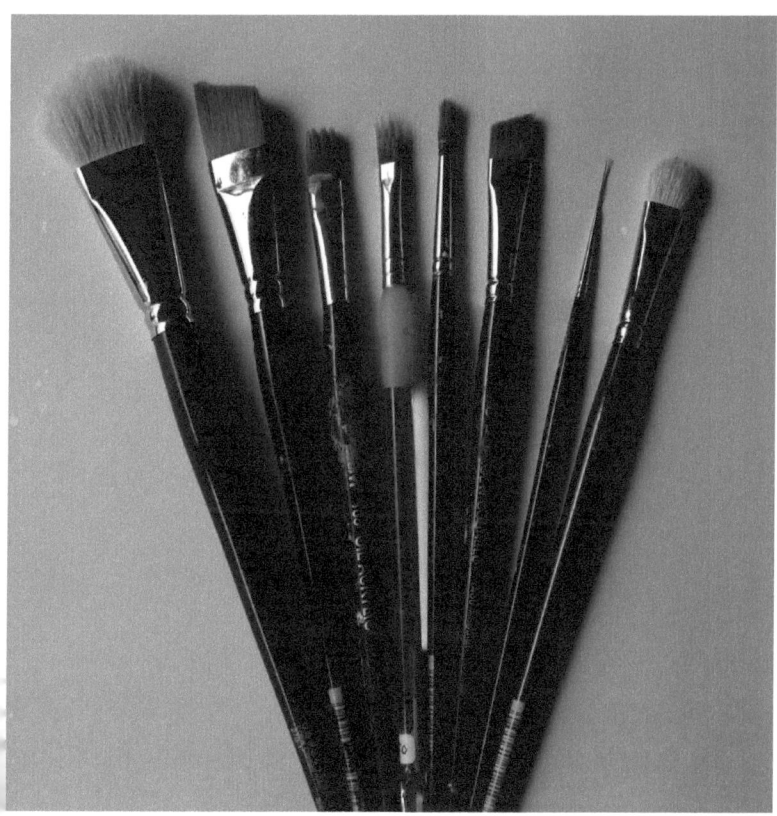

Paper Palette

Next on your list is "paper palette", a special paper that does not absorb water, it is used to "unload" the excess of color from the angular brush while shading or highlighting; You will be able to find paper palette in albums of about 40 sheets each, which appears as a white lucid sheet. I recommend reusing the same sheet up to three times, as the properties of the paper remain the same and it is the more ecologic choice. To clean it simply cleanse the trace of shading/highlighting with a damp paper towel.

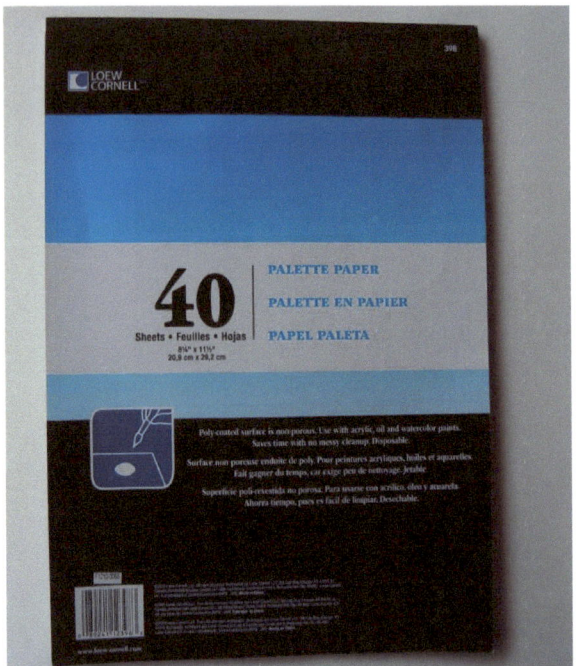

Acrylic Colors

Almost all country painting artists use the "Americana deco art" acrylic colors, which will allow you to easily follow artists patterns without mistakes. Americana colors can be used on any surface with the right primer; There is an infinite range of colors, trust me, you will fall in love very quickly, you can of course mix the colors to obtain the perfect nuance you are looking for. There are colors that you will use on almost every project, such as black and white and so on, which are sold in bigger bottles. Depending on the usage, and Americana acrylic color tube can last you years. Always remember to close the lid of your bottle because, as I said before, acrylic colors dry quickly

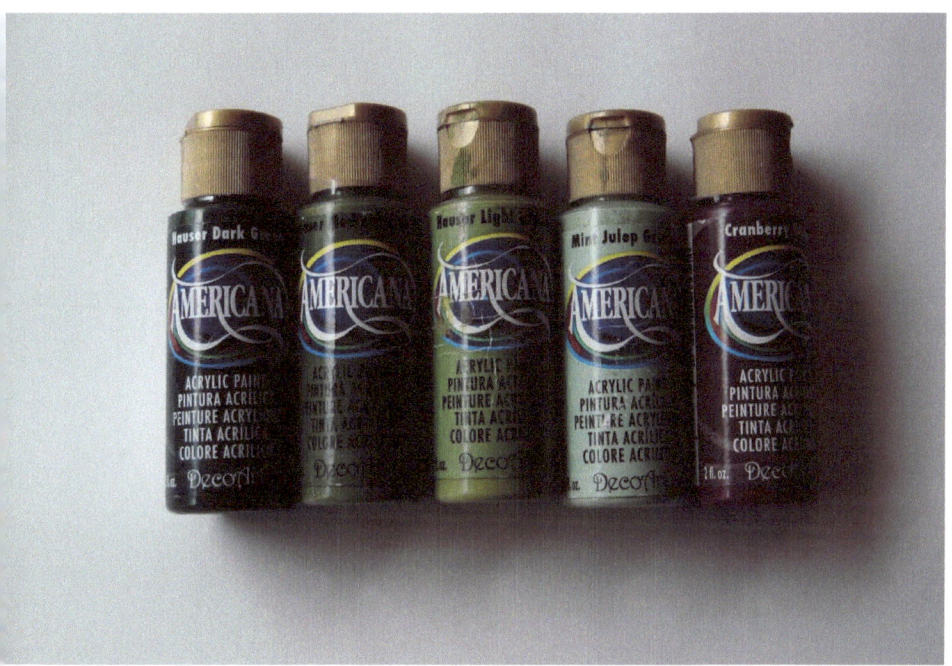

Brush Washer

Then we have the brush washer, which is simply a plastic water holder with two sections, one for clean water the other with ribs on the bottom to help scrub the paint off of your paintbrush, and some of these holders also have little spaces to hold your brushes on the sides. It does not sound like much, but trust me, the ribs on the bottom of these washers are very useful to give you a clean brush ready to re use.

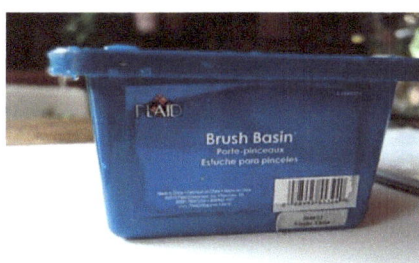

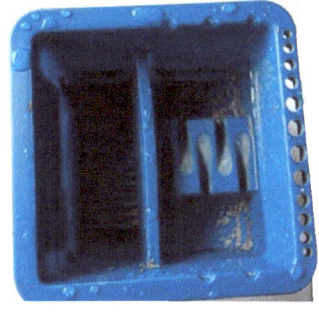

Paper Towels

And least but not last some plain paper towels, don't use tissues, they leave a paper residue on your brushes. The paper towel sheet is normally folded in half and then half again, and deeply wet on the middle with clean water; you will need it to "dry" the brush after cleaning it in your washer. For example, when you finished shading, you clean your brush in the washer and then pad it on the wet paper towel, the brush is now ready to re use.

CHAPTER 2

Techniques

Let's examine the essential brushes you will need to start painting: the "Loew Cornell angular brush" and the "Loew Cornell Maxine mop" for shading and highlighting (don't be alarmed, we will get to the terminology soon). All the brushes come in 3 to 4 sizes each, and you can generally buy them as part of a set, so you can always have the perfect brush for your current project, no matter how small or large!

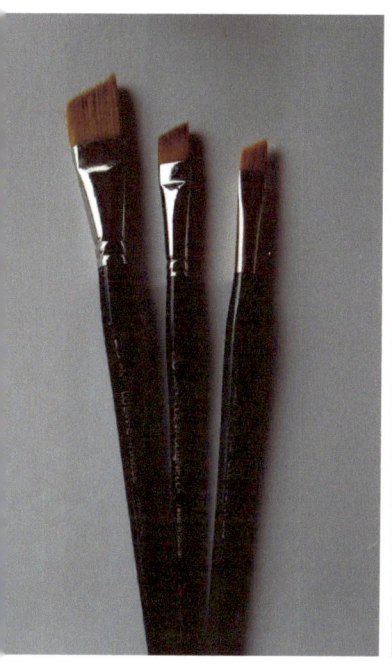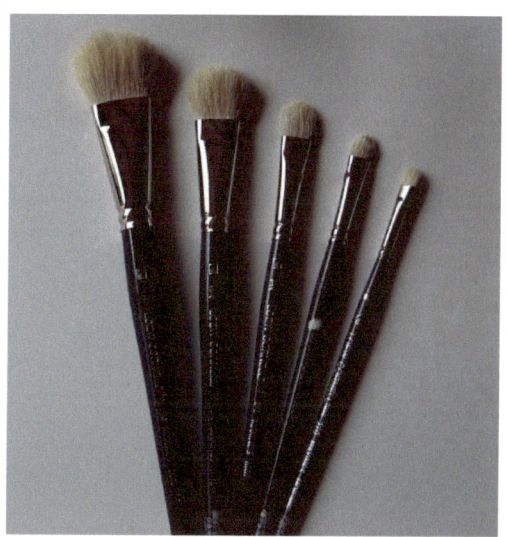

The angular brush depicted on the left is used to Shade and highlight all the singles details of you project: Shading means giving that subject "shade" , transforming the object from 2 dimensional to 3 dimensional.

The mop brush depicted on the right is used to "mop up" the excess water from the shading process.

If the subject has a "shade" it will have a "highlight" as well, highlighting means giving in subject its light. The shade and light will be positioned at the opposite sides from each other, and they will positioned on the subject depending on where the subject itself is located in respect to the sun light.

You will also read of "basecoating" or basecoat: the basecoat is the base color of each ingular part of your project. Choosing the basecoat color will allow you to decide which color to use to shade and highlight, for example if I were to paint a leaf I would basecoat it with "houser medium green", then shade it with "houser dark green" and afterwards highlight it with "houser light green".

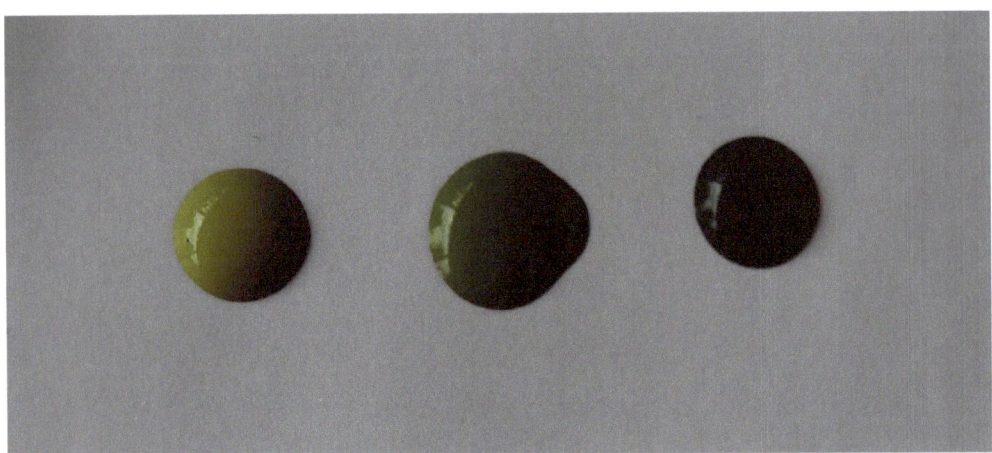

Now let me show you how to use both brushes

Angular Brush... used for shading and highlighting

Simply sink your brush in clean water, and then take off the exceeding water by gently pressing both sides of the brush on the side of your water bowl.

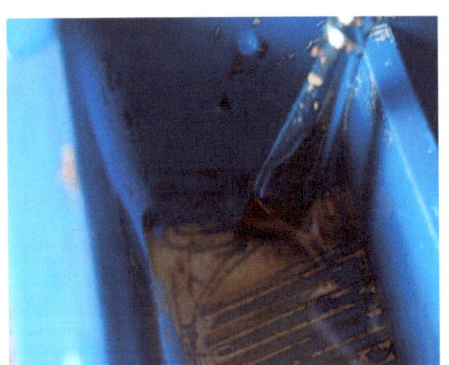 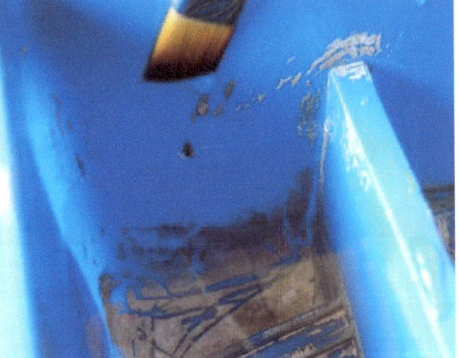

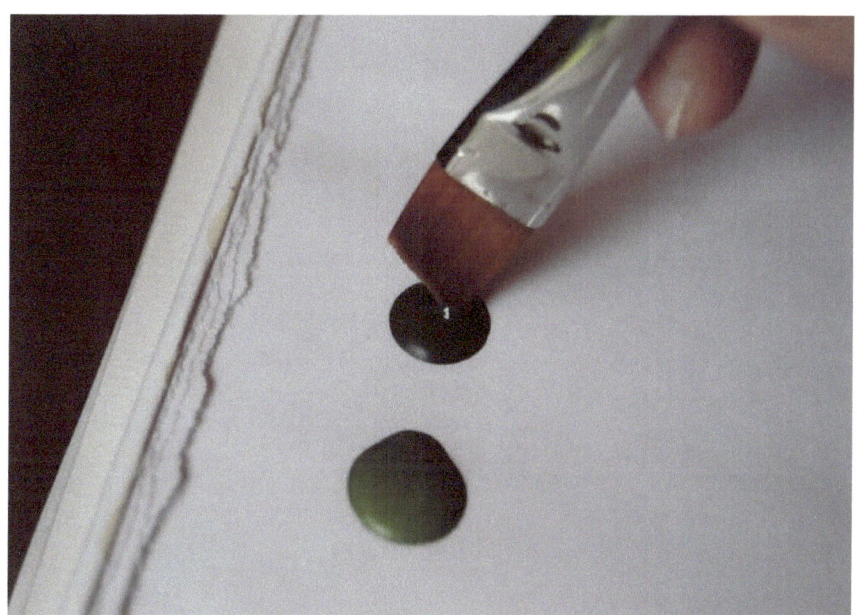

Dip the tip of the brush in your color, being careful to leave the "tail" of the brush clean.

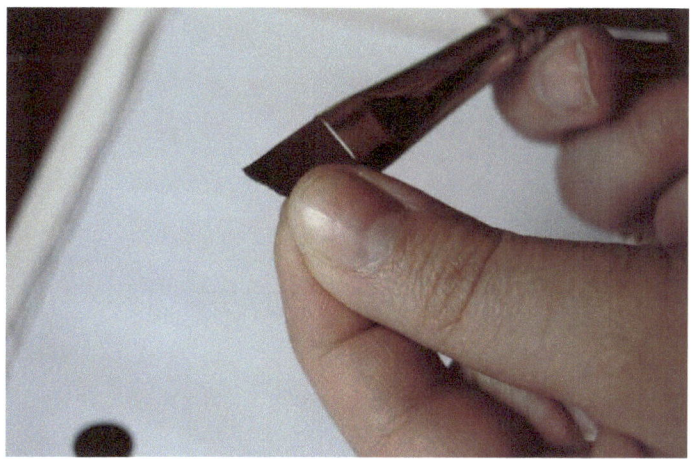

Now draw semi circles or straight lines on the paper palette pressing down first one side of the brush then the other, going up and down while being careful to follow the previous line.

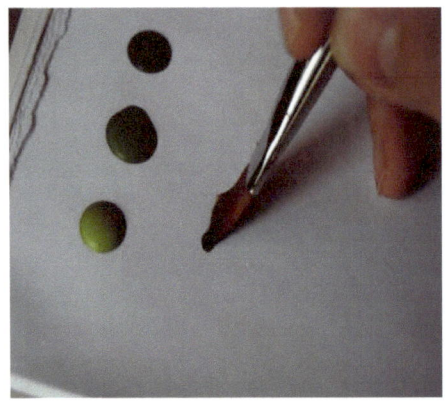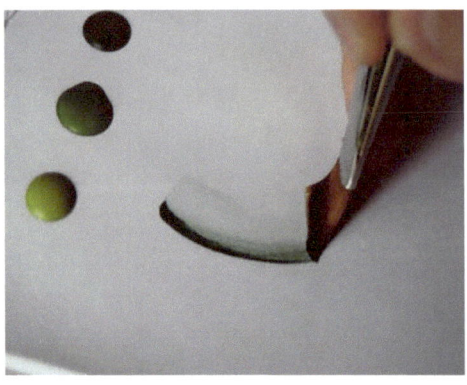

Now your brush is ready to be used to shade or to highlight your project,

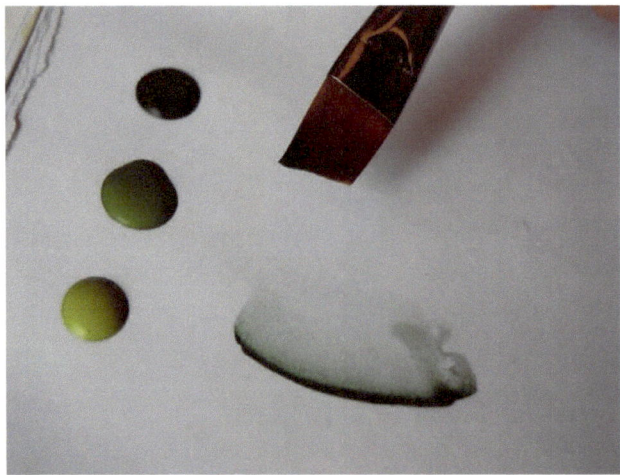

Position the tip of the brush facing the side you want to shade, and gently pressing down the brush, start shading, it does not have to be a straight line, you can do multiple passes with the shade multiple times. (Feel free to rotate the project to any angle that you find comfortable). When the results satisfy you, gently push up and down the mop on the shade to absorb the extra water remained on the shade itself, doing so will give a "powder look" to you shade.

The process of shading is simply giving an object its shadow, for example: the country girl on the right picture has her shadows, the lower part of the hair, the face, the collar, the apron and of every square or her shirt has been shaded, giving it a shadow means transforming the object from 2 dimensional (first picture with only the basecoat) to 3 diminsional (second picture). To give each element of your project (hair , face ecc) a shadow , you simply have to decide where you want the light to be in that moment, in this case the light is on top of the country girl (as it normally is)

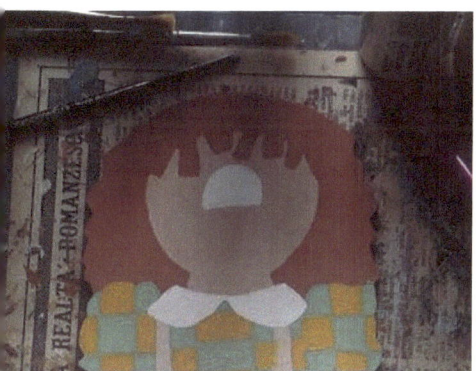 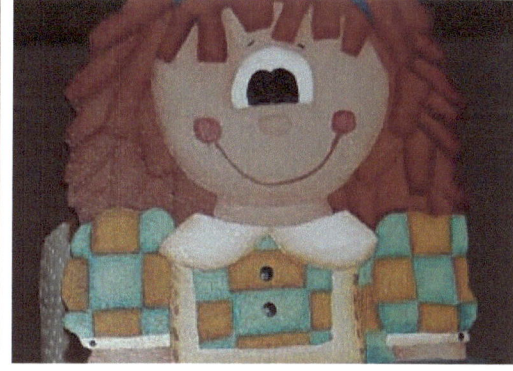

The same exact procedure is used for highlighting.

Remember it is always best to get the full set of brushes in multiple sizes, both for the mops and the angular brushes, as you will soon notice that each project might need multiple measures of the same brush, depending on the width of the shade you want to obtain. Now, we talked about "basecoating", "shading" and "highlighting", we talked about essential brushes like the "angular brush" and the "mop", are you ready to take it to the next level?

There are other useful brushes you will need in order to be able to fully enjoy country painting, such as the Crescent Loew Cornell brush used for "dry brushing", it is a very useful brush to obtain a non specific highlight or shade on your object or for example to have nice round rosy cheeks on your subjects.

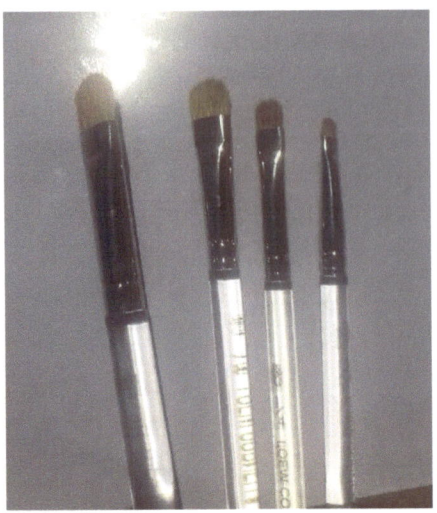

They are very useful to use, just remember they DO NOT like water, so while using them do not wet them.

Simply choose the color you want to use, pour a little bit on your plate and sink your brush in it, dip it a couple of times in the color pool so the bristles get most of it, then get a paper towel and "clean" the brush on it applying a bit of force, doing this will push the color inside the bristles but take off the exceeding color on the tip of the brush, keep brushing back and forth on the paper towel, as if you were coloring the paper towel, and when the stroke on the paper towel looks faded, then the brush is "charged"

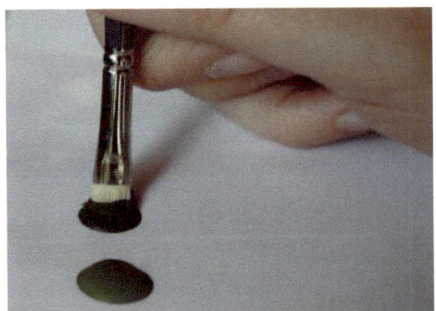

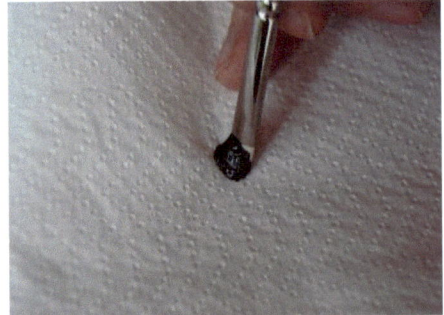

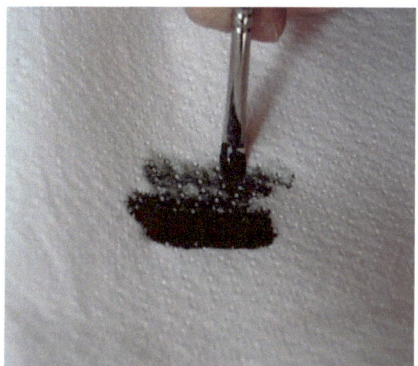

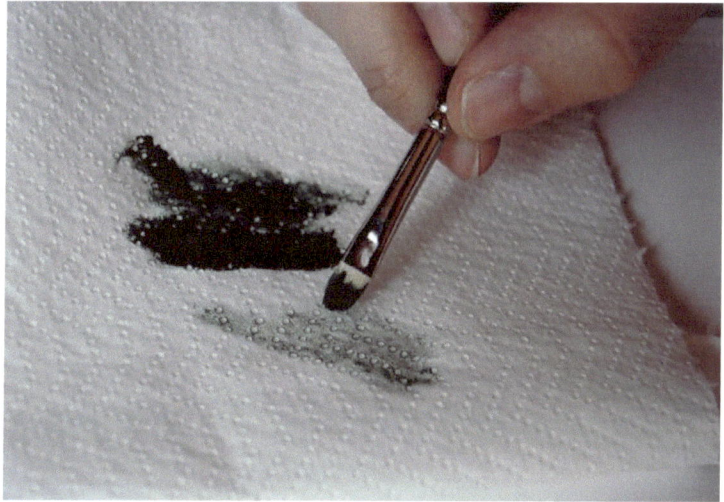

Now, very very gently use it on your project, apply the color with circular, vertical or horizontal movements. The more force you apply to the brush, the stronger the mark will be.

Here is an example on how you can use this brushes, the cheeks of this owl have been colored with this technique.

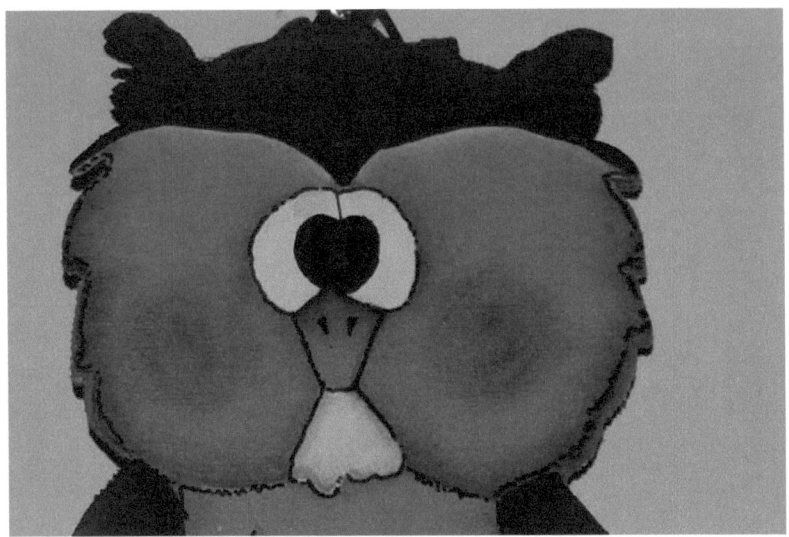

Another fun brush to use is the "Royal aqualon wisp" , this brush is indicated if you need thin strokes of color, which are often used to paint the fur of animals or grass, or even straw.

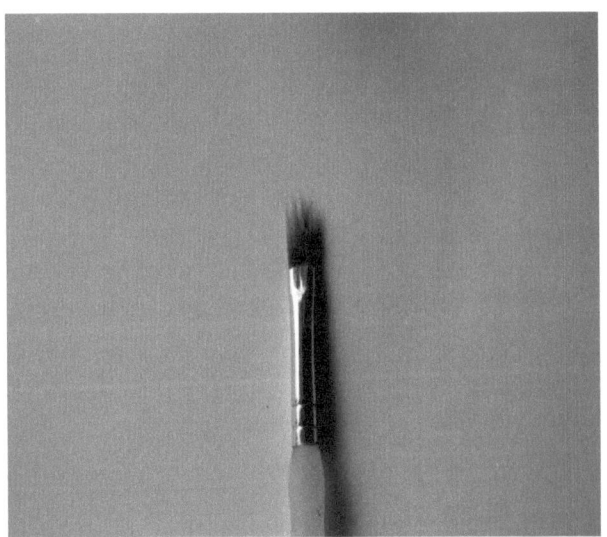

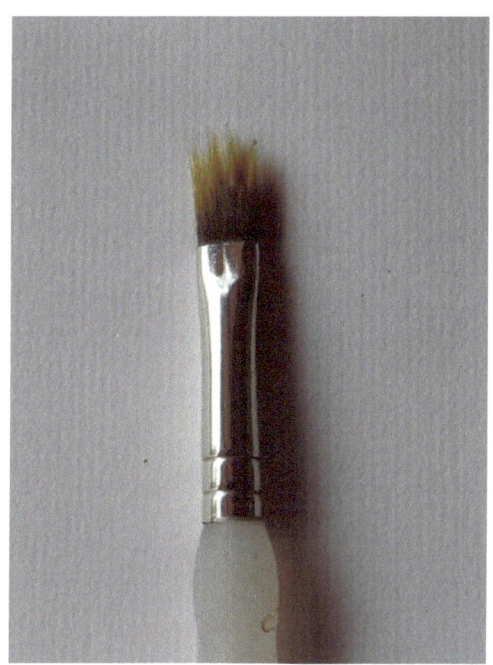

To use this brush simply choose the color you want to use, pour it into your plate and sink the brush in the color, firmly pushing the brush down on the plate, you will see the bristles opening up in a fan, then firmly push the brush down in a zone of the plate with no color to take off the excess paint and your brush is now ready.

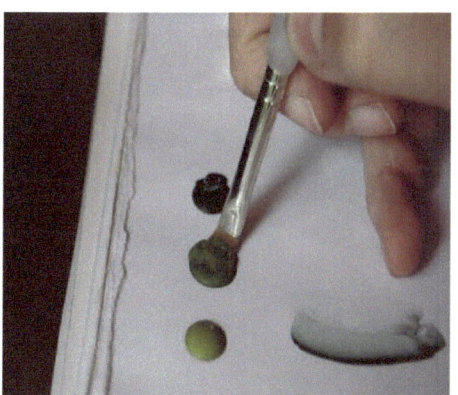 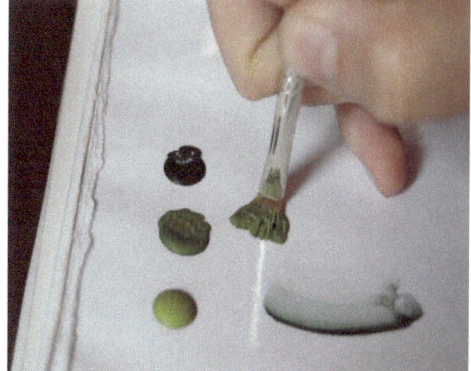

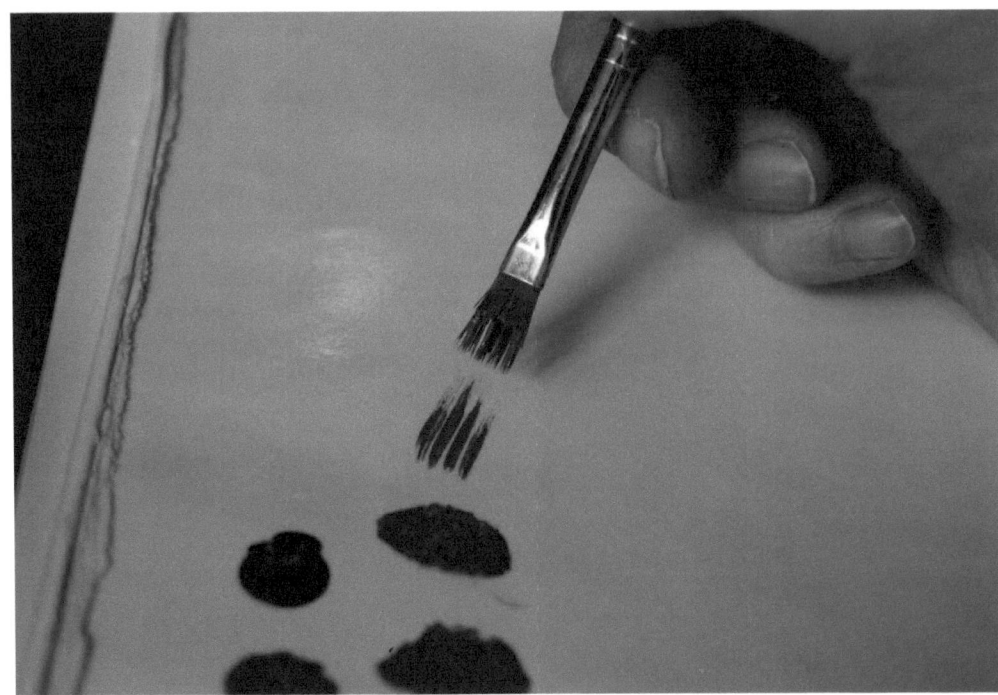

Remember to be very gentle while using this brush to create the strokes, the lighter the pressure applied, the thinner the strokes will be (less pressure applied will result in thinner strokes) and will look better. Here we have an example

.

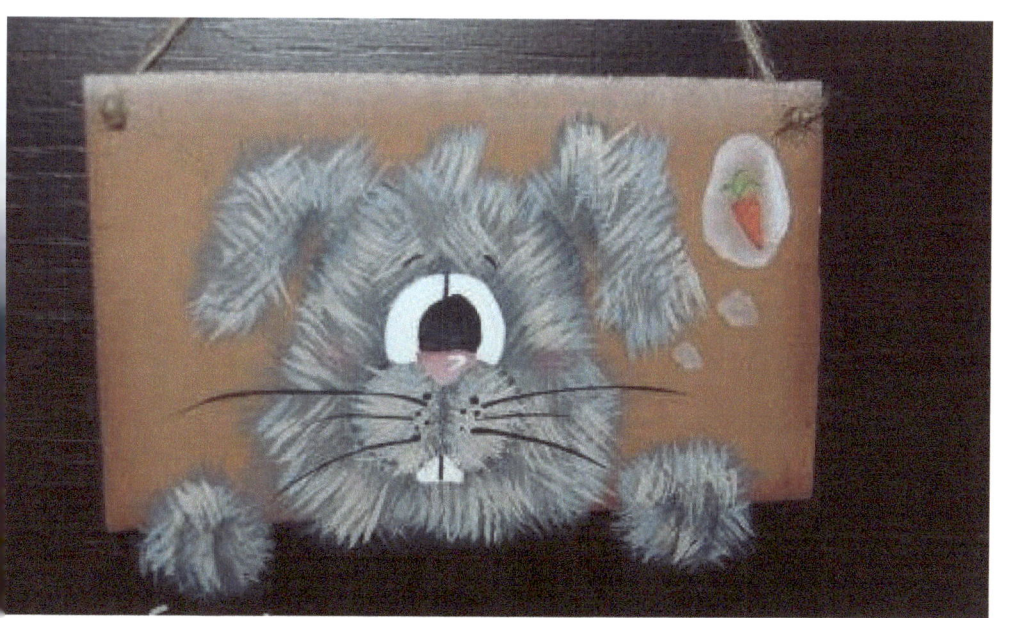

Now you have learned the bases of country painting, there are more techniques but it is best to learn the basics, practice until you are confident and then experiment with the ess used brushes.

CHAPTER 3

Mistakes

Shade /Highlight

Not to worry, almost anything can be erased and repainted, if you make a mistake with your shade or highlight, simply wet a piece of cotton in clean water, take off the exceeding water from the tip and wipe your shade or highlight right off.

Dry brush

If you put too much pressure and the highlight is too marked, you can use the same erasing technique as for shading, even though sometimes it is simpler to basecoat the part of your project with the mistake.

CHAPTER 4

Practice

ARTURO THE OWL

BASE:

ANTIQUE WHITE: Body and muzzle

BURNT SIENNA: Wings and head

WHITE: Beard and eyes

SPICY MUSTARD: Beak

BLACK: Pupils and eyebrows

MILK CHOCOLATE: Branch

SHADES:: Shade the inside of the wings and the lower part of the ears and forehead.

RAW SIENNA + L. BUTTERMILK: Highlight the outside of the wings and the upper part of ears and forehead.

RAW SIENNA: Shade all around the outside part of the body of the owl, and shade around eyes, beak, beard and delineate the muzzle, with the "float" technique (explained below) create some "W" s on the owl's body to simulate plumage.

LIGHT BUTTERMILK: Highlight under the eyebrows and under the ears and muzzle.

BURNT SIENNA: Shade the upper part of the beak (the part connected to the eyes)

BURNT UMBER: Shade all around the outside of the branch, "float" the details on the branch (grains and circles)

RED IRON OXIDE: "Dry brush" the cheeks

FINISHING:

Screw the "L" shaped nails on the branch to be able to hang your keys and another nail on the back of the project to be able to hang it.

With a black marker (very thin tip) outline the entire owl and branch, delineating paws, forehead, face, beard, beak, and inner body plumage.

Float: Technique similar to the Shading/highlighting but that uses the angular brush without removing the exceeding water therefore using a very wet angular brush.

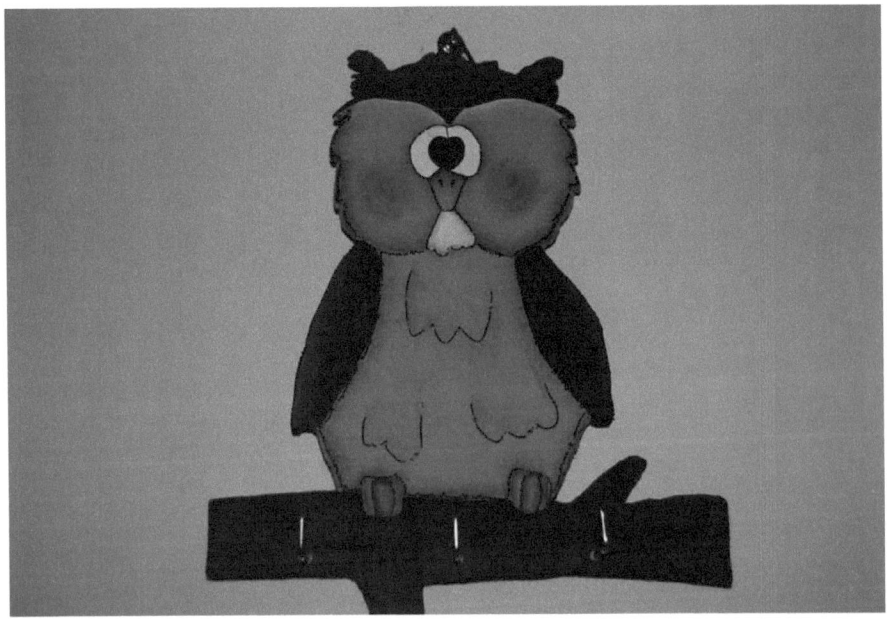

PENNY the Pig

BASE:

FLESH TONE: Body of the Pig

COUNTRY RED: Scarf

WHITE: Dots

BLACK and WHITE: Eyes and pupils

DARK CHOCOLATE: Hoofs

HOUSER MEDIUM GREEN: Grass

SHADES::

SHADING FLESH: Shade around the outside of ears and the muzzle and eyes, Shade around the face and under the chin, shade around the body and create the arms of the pig, shade under the scarf.

SABLE BROWN: Shade the inside of the nose and create the nostrils, shade the inside of the ears

WHITE: Highlight the top of the ears, of the nose and of the head of the pig

HERITAGE BRICK: Shade the bottom inside of the scarf, the top of the ribbon and the inside of the knot, shade the inside of the scarf (where the scarf turns around the shoulder of the pig)

FIERY RED: Highlight the top of the scarf, highlight the bottom of the ribbon and the top of the knot.

SOFT BLACK: Shade all around the hoofs

SABLE BROWN: Dry brush the inside of the hoofs

AVOGADO: Shade the top part of the grass, where it touches the hoofs

FINISHING:

Glue all the pieces of Penny the Pig together (body + hoofs)

With little screws and metal "L" supports screw in the wood base of the book end.

Spray everything with transparent finishing for wood.

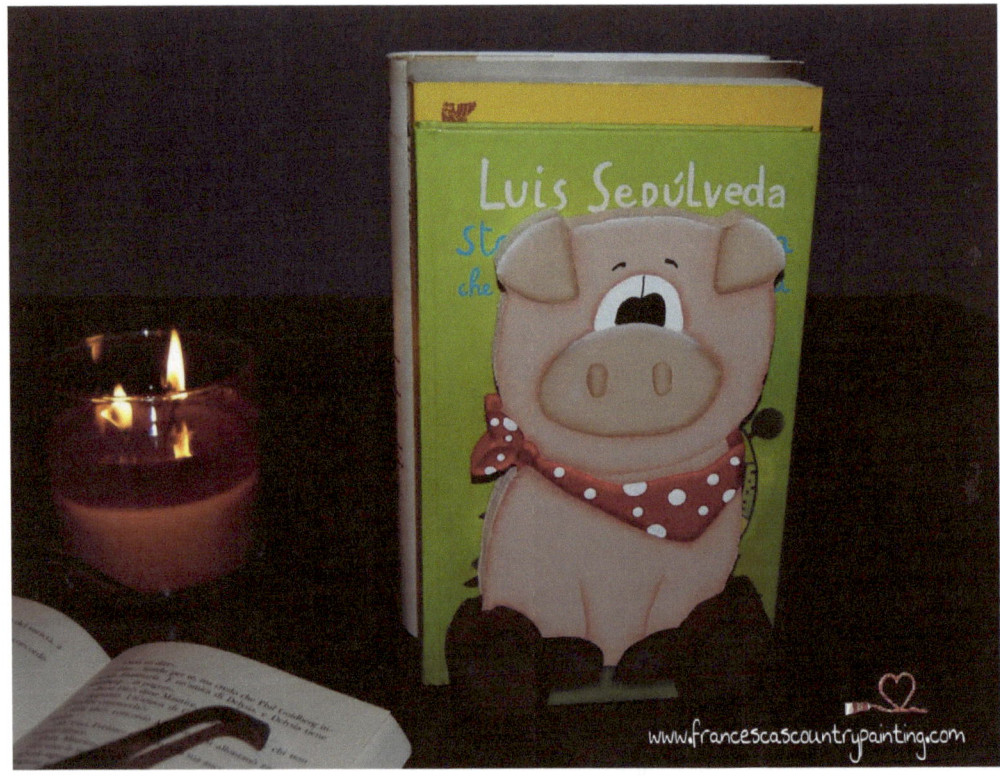

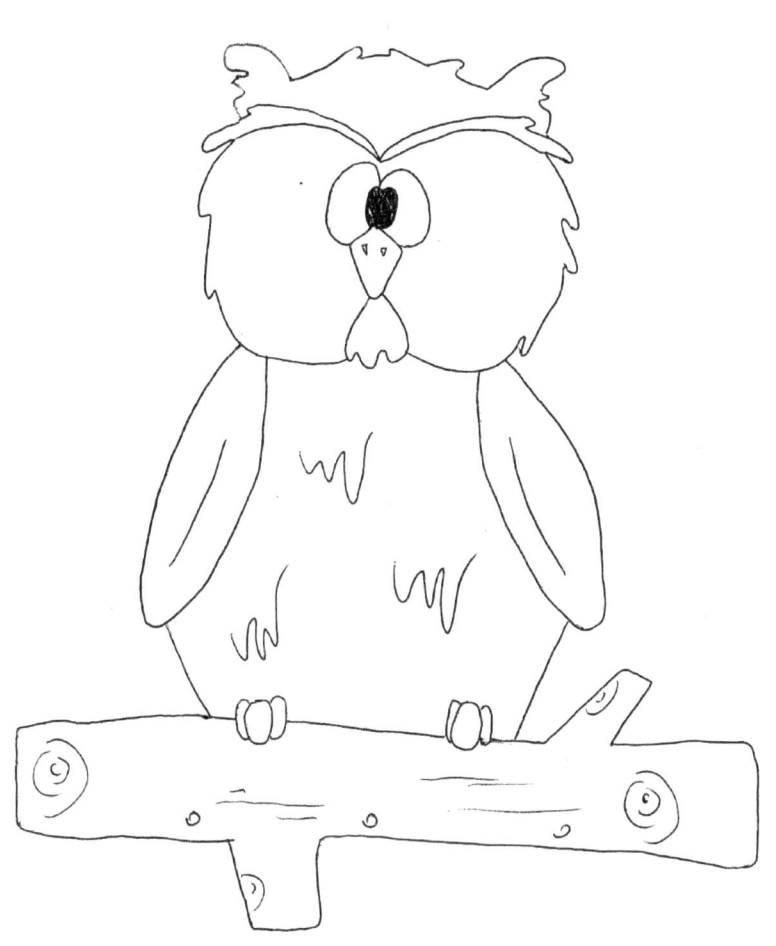

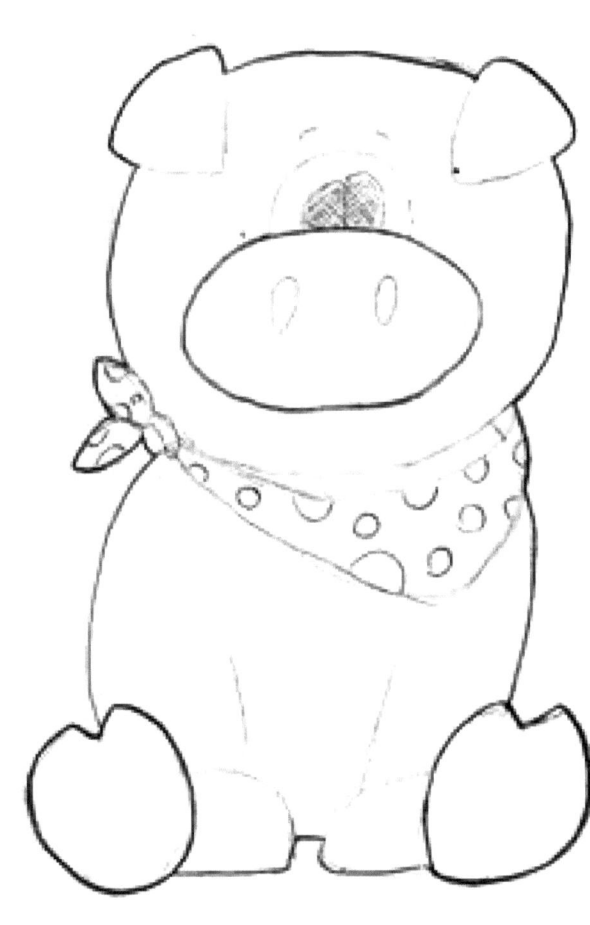

www.ingramcontent.com/pod-product-compliance
Lightning Source LLC
Chambersburg PA
CBHW041619180526
45159CB00002BC/930